The Rockies: Wildlife

A pictorial guide to the wildlife of the Canadian Rockies.

The Rockies are home to a rich diversity of spectacular wild animals, most of which are featured in this volume. Colorful, wide-format images capture the personality, characteristics and habitat of the wilderness creatures of the high country.

National park wildlife sometimes seem tame and friendly, but they are wild and often unpredictable. When cornered, startled or fearful for the safety of their young, wild animals may attack human.

Elk, coyote, bears and other animals have been known to injure people in recent years; the photographs in this book allow the viewer to enjoy the wilderness creatures of the Rockies safely.

Photographic studies by George Brybycin:

The High Rockies
Colourful Calgary
Our Fragile Wilderness
The Rocky Mountains
Banff National Park
Jasper National Park
Colourful Calgary II
Wildlife in the Rockies
Rocky Mountain Symphony
Enchanted Wilderness
Wilderness Odyssey
Rocky Mountain Symphony II
Romance of the Rockies
Calgary – The Sunshine City
The Living Rockies
Cosmopolitan Calgary
Banff and Jasper N.P.
The Rockies: Wildlife
The Majestic Rockies

Front Cover: Columbian Ground Squirrels

Text Editor: Kevin Van Tighem
Design: George Brybycin
Printed and bound in Singapore by
Kim Hup Lee Printing Co Pte Limited

Copyright © 1993 by G B Publishing

First Edition 1993

ISBN 0-919029-19-1 Paperback

For current list, please write to:
GB PUBLISHING, Box 6292, Station D,
Calgary, Alberta Canada T2P 2C9

The Rockies: Wildlife

Photographs by
GEORGE BRYBYCIN

G B PUBLISHING

A hoary marmot (Marmota caligata) on its front doorstep.

Bull elk (Cervus elaphus) become highly agitated and dangerously unpredictable during the fall rutting season.

One of the first harbingers of spring, the Glacier lily (Erythronium grandiflorum)
emerges from the edges of melting snow banks in June.

The Canadian lynx (Lynx canadensis) is one of four species of lynx in the world, and the only one that lives in the Canadian Rockies.
It ranges at various elevations but is most common in forested valleys where it seeks its main prey, the snowshoe hare.
Its long whiskers and tufted ears are attractive and distinctive characteristics.

The gray jay (Perisoreus canadensis), smallest member of the Corvidae, or crow family, is commonly found in coniferous forests.

Willow ptarmigan (Lagopus lagopus) is found at timeberline from Jasper National Park north.

Left: Related to the sea eagles, the bald eagle (Haliaeetus leucocephalus) is the best-known of North America's two eagle species.

Alpine flowers on the north slope of Quartz Hill, just west of Citadel Pass.

The wolf (Canis lupus) is the largest member of the Canidae (dog family) in temperate North America.
An efficient and intelligent predator, the wolf adjusts its breeding habits
in response to food availability.

Delicious and pretty, the wild strawberry (Frgaria glauca) is found throughout the Rockies.

The largest of the cat family, the cougar, or mountain lion (Felis concolor) is a secretive hunter rarely seen in daylight.

The shy and omnivorous red fox (Vulpes vulpes) is found in the forested, low-elevation valleys. Its summer diet includes vegetation, insects and rodents; in winter it eats birds, small mammals and carrion.

A member of the deer family, the elk (Cervus canadensis) is also known as ''wapiti'' – an Indian name referring to its pale-colored rump. Mature bull elk gather large harems of cows during the rutting season.

A large relative of the woodchuck, the hoary marmot (Marmota caligata) inhabits alpine meadows, seeks safety among boulders, and hibernates in winter.

The spectacular colors of the alpine world near Bow Summit.
Observation Peak (3174 m.) in the background.

Bighorn sheep (Ovis canadensis) are found in many parts of the Rocky Mountains. They feed in high-country meadows and escape danger by fleeing into nearby crags. They spend winters in windy places or at lower elevations where the snow remains shallow. Farther north in the Rockies, the related Stone sheep is found, and further north yet another cousin – the Dall sheep – inhabits the heights.

Deep in the mountain wilderness at the foot of Pharaoh Peak (2711 m.), Mummy Lake lies surrounded by timberline beauty. Banff National Park.

The agile and fearless acrobat of the heights, a mountain goat (Oreamnos americanus)
and kid overlooking the Athabasca River, Jasper National Park.

22

Kananaskis Country; the Opal Range. This is what survives of the once-pristine Kananaskis valley.
Large scale developments have damaged the northern part of the valley.

The world's largest deer, the moose (Alces alces). Moose browse on twigs and foliage, but in the summer they also feed on aquatic vegetation. Weighing 500 to 600 kg., a cow moose consumes up to 30 kg. of food per day.

Of the fourteen species of goose, the Canada goose (Branta canadensis)
is the best-known in North America.

*Canada goose (Branta canadensis). Proud and vigilant parents with
a record brood of twenty nine goslings.*

The prettiest of jays, Stellar's jay (Cyanocitta stelleri)
is found mostly on the western side of the Rockies.

Black bear (Euarctos americanus) is the most widespread North American member of the Ursidae (bear family). It occupies most forested parts of the continent where it leads a shy and solitary life, feeding on vegetation, berries and anything it can find. When black bears become accustomed to humans, they can become aggressive and dangerous.

Deep into the wilderness, above Geraldine Lakes, a high pass opens to the south. The alpine tundra and lower meadows are frequented by mountain caribou, grizzly bears, wolves and very few humans.

Cow moose (Alces alces) browsing on fresh spring willow shoots.
Notice the partially shed winter coat.

Mule deer (Odocoileus hemionus) is found throughout western North America in forests and prairie. Large dark-rimmed ears, tawny-gray coat, and black-tipped tail distinguish this deer from its smaller cousin, the white-tailed deer.

32

The icy waters draining Lake Oesa cascade cheerfully down towards Lake O'Hara, in Yoho National Park.
Odaray Mountain dominates the horizon.

An inhabitant of the high alpine meadows, a hoary marmot
(Marmota caligata) at a family picnic.

The agile mountian goat (Oreamnos americanus) inhabits craggy slopes where it finds food and safety.
Its long thick coat enables it to spend winter days foraging on open, wind-swept slopes before
taking shelter from the night winds among high crags.

Nothing is more profoundly wild and thrilling than a wolf's howl. The largest of wild dogs, the wolf (Canis lupus) is a majestic and powerful symbol of Canadian wilderness.

Although it has few natural enemies, a cow moose (Alces alces) remains vigilant, watching and listening for wolves which can trap moose in deep snow and eventually kill them.

The introverted, slow-moving porcupine (Erethizon dorsatum) can teach a very painful lesson to anyone who dares to disturb it. Those 30,000 barbed quills persuade most intruders to leave this prickly creature alone.

Moose (Alces alces) can weigh up to 700 kg., making them the largest deer in the world.

*Plains and wood bison (Bison bison) once inhabited the entire North American continent. Bison have been hunted,
harvested and managed out of existence except for a few small populations which survive in a few National Parks,
paddocks and zoos. These are the heaviest ungulates ("ungula" means hoof) in North America.*

An idyll on an alpine meadow: mating grizzly bears (Ursus arctos). This majestic bear ranges from the alpine meadows to the river valleys. It is omnivorous, feeding mostly on vegetation, and hibernates for five to six months. Grizzlies must be treated with great respect; they can be extremely dangerous when approached at close range.

There are six distinct forms of reindeer or caribou; in the northern Rockies one of these, the mountain caribou (Rangifer tarandus montanus) survives as an endangered species in several areas. Unlike their northern cousins, mountain caribou do not migrate long distances. After spending summer in the high meadows, they move down to the old-growth forests of lower valleys for the winter to feed on lichens and shelter from freezing winds.

Engelmann spruce and golden larch forest around picturesque
Elizabeth Lake. Mount Assiniboine Provincial Park, B.C.

A high altitude dweller, the Pika (Ochotona princeps) of the Ochotonidae family. This gregarious creature communicates with others by loud, high-pitched beeps.

The American marten (Martes americana), a member of the Mustelidae (weasel family). Martens live in old conifer forests where they feed upon small rodents and birds.

A member of the dogwood family, bunchberry (Cornus canadensis) finds the tree trunk a hospitable place to live.

There are several forms of wild sheep in North America. The Dall sheep (Ovis dalli) is the northern-most, ranging through the mountains of Yukon, Northwest Territories and Alaska. This snow-white, thin-horned species is smaller than the bighorn sheep of the Canadian Rockies.

White globeflower (Trollius albiflorus) is commonly found in wet alpine meadows and along streams. They are among the first harbingers of spring, often emerging out from under the melting snow.

The most widespread wild dog in Canada, the coyote (Canis latrans) is common in the Rockies. Coyotes feed mostly on small rodents and birds, but are also very efficient scavengers of carrion.

East of Boulder Pass and Ptarmigan Lake, the alpine wilderness around Baker Lake is home to a diversity of wildlife, including the grizzly bear. The Sawback Range forms the backdrop.

Elk, or wapiti (Cervus elaphus), spend summers in high valleys and alpine meadows, wintering at lower elevations where the snow remains shallow.

*Above and left: Mule deer (Odocoileus hemionus) are the characteristic deer of western Canada.
Note the different colours and phases of antler development in these bucks.*

A Dall sheep (Ovis dalli) lamb roams the northern alpine meadows on a sunny summer day.

Wolves (Canis lupus) have been typecast as the ''big, bad wolf'' of legend; here they prove otherwise.

One of the most beautiful of Canada's wilderness flowers, the yellow lady's slipper (Cypripedium calceolus) was once common in the Banff area but has now been exterminated by excessive flower picking. Long ago, H. Ellis said: "The sun, moon and stars would have disappeared long ago if they had happened to be within the reach of predatory human hands."

*Grizzly bear (Ursus arctos). This majestic bear ranges from the alpine meadows to the river valleys.
It is omnivorous and hibernates for five to six months.*

Above: A magnificent bull elk (Cervus elaphus) at the forest edge in late autumn.
Left: The largest of the cat family, the cougar (Felis concolor) is also known as mountain lion.
Although common in the Rockies, this secretive nocturnal hunter is seldom seen.

*East Lyell Glacier, west of Howse River and Glacier Lake, is the
main source of the Glacier River. Banff National Park.*

Columbian ground squirrel (Spermophilus colombianus). These familiar, handsome faces can be seen at roadside campgrounds, in forest clearings or in high, alpine meadows. Hibernating from September to April, ground squirrels sometimes fall prey to grizzly bears who dig them up.

Dall sheep (Ovis dalli) in the high alpine tundra of the far northern Rockies.

Clark's nutcracker (Nucifraga columbiana), a jay closely related to crows, is common in many parts of the Rockies.

The Author's Call for Environmental Wisdom

George Brybycin has a passion for nature, wilderness and the mountains. He spends most of his life exploring, photographing, admiring and learning from nature in his home, the Canadian Rockies.

George has travelled widely in search of adventure and challenges throughout the mountainous regions of the Canadian and American West. His North American endeavors have been crowned with trips to the Yukon, Alaska, Arctic coast and islands of British Columbia.

Born and educated in Poland, George has travelled extensively in Europe, Asia, South America and Africa, including visits to many national parks and an ascent of Mt. Kilimanjaro.

Young George joined the boy scouts, and like many others fortunate enough to enjoy direct contact with nature at an early age, became a dedicated outdoorsman. Summer and winter camps in the great outdoors marked him for life as a passionate mountain man and naturalist. He earned his ranks as a mountaineer in the spectacular and pristine Polish Carpathian and Tatra Mountains where wolves, bear, deer, chamois, wild boar and lynx still roam free . . . a wonderful world.

Well, it was.

After seeing the smoke, polluted water and mountains of garbage in Germany, Japan and parts of the United States; the devastated jungles of Amazonia and the islands of Indonesia; and the almost totally-destroyed forests in some parts of Africa, George has come to a sad conclusion. "The world is being run by unscrupulous, shrewd and narrow-minded people whose only aim is to make one more dollar, no matter how."

To stop the destruction of nature, George suggests global action that starts with each individual's decisions. "Do not buy useless, and harmful, gimmicks and gadgets. Above all, avoid overpackaged and disposable items which hungry, irresponsible industries produce and push on us, while corrupted and passive governments turn a blind eye."

"Live a humble, simple, natural and non-materialistic life. What matters is who you are, what are your principles and moral convictions; not what you possess."

George says that above all, we need to reduce the uncontrolled growth of the world's populations or we will almost certainly drown in dirty water, pollution and mountains of garbage. To those who feel he is an alarmist, George points to examples he has personally seen. The once-blue Danube and Rhine Rivers, for example, are now almost black, flowing sewers. One is considered fortunate to glimpse Mount Fuji through the thick, ever-present smog in the Tokyo area. Lake Erie is unsafe for swimming; it has become an industrial waste reservoir. Thousands of people die annually in Mexico City from horrific air pollution. In the eastern United States, many beaches are closed due to raw sewage.

"Just too many people everywhere," says George.

The situation is worse than most of us realize. The very air is polluted, causing acid rain and damaging the ozone layer. Surface and ground water, increasingly, are being found to be polluted; so are the oceans. What is left unpolluted? Very little; the problems are global.

"Take a stand," says George Brybycin, a man who has known and loved the richness of nature, and witnessed man's assaults on it. Do your small part today, or our children may never have the opportunity to see a green forest, a bird, blue sky or drink pure, clean water.